T
abc

CW00919228

ex libris

Candlestick Press

Published by:
Candlestick Press,
Diversity House, 72 Nottingham Road, Arnold, Nottingham NG5 6LF
www.candlestickpress.co.uk

Design and typesetting by Craig Twigg

Printed by Ratcliff & Roper Print Group, Nottinghamshire, UK

Selection and Introduction © George Szirtes, 2011

Cover illustration © Paul Catherall 'Bridge Lime'
www.paulcatherall.com

Candlestick Press monogram © Barbara Shaw, 2008

First Published 2011
Reprinted 2012, 2014, 2020

ISBN 978 1 907598 04 3

Acknowledgements:

Candlestick Press thanks Alexander Perkins and Bloodaxe Books for
permission to reprint Elizabeth Bartlett, 'Underground' from *Collected
Poems* (Bloodaxe Books, 2010); and Sarah Wardle and Bloodaxe Books
for permission to reprint 'The Capital' from *Fields Away* (Bloodaxe Books,
2003). Thanks are also due to Carcanet Press for permission to reprint Elaine
Feinstein, 'Homecoming' from *Collected Poems and Translations* (Carcanet
Press, 2002). AN Stencl, 'A Linden Tree in Whitechapel Street' translated from
the Yiddish by Joseph Leftwich is reprinted by kind permission of Mrs Miriam
Becker, and WS Graham, 'The Night City', taken from *New Collected Poems*
(Faber and Faber, 2005) by kind permission of Michael Snow.

Thanks are also due to Lorraine Mariner for her researches.

Where poets are no longer living, their dates are given.

Introduction

To arrive in the private London of the suburbs in 1957
was very different from arriving in the public London of
monuments and grand shops. Having lived in the paranoid
austerity of post-war central Budapest it was the smallness of
suburban streets, their quietness, self-containment, and slightly
prim yet distinctly jaunty air of reserve that struck me.

I was only eight and we were moving slowly through the
refugee path of betterment, from poor suburb to middling
suburb over a period of some ten years. Central London
– Wordsworth's, Shakespeare's, Dr Johnson's, Sherlock
Holmes's, Jack the Ripper's and everybody else's myth-
London – was an excursion, a trip on the tube to, say, Charlotte
Square for those later Sunday lunches at Schmidt's, or for
a half-dutiful, half-exciting visit to the Science Museum, or
the Zoo. I knew nothing of Soho or Bloomsbury or Hangover
Square, the East End, the Docks or any of the secrets of the
river, not till later, from books or from films. They were
exotica. It was like the thick fogs that still prevailed then. It
was smog that held the idea together.

And yet there was something – a feeling, a trace – a kind of
inner map that settled in the nervous system as a way of being.
London was more potential than reality in this sense. Inducted
into the ways of bus-spotting at the age of ten I dreamed of
getting all those buses travelling all those red routes into every
part of London. Exploring the full extent of the city would
be an intoxicating adventure and when the journeys were
completed there would be something of infinite value at the
end, a knowledge of self, space and society. It would be like
going to the ends of the earth. It would be as if one had learned
the world. Even now, travelling the tube or waiting at a station,
the world seems possible in all its stunning variety: the world
heading back to its infinite number of homes to dream itself
over and over again, right into the core of things.

George Szirtes

Composed upon Westminster Bridge
September 3, 1802

Earth has not anything to show more fair:
Dull would he be of soul who could pass by
A sight so touching in its majesty:
This City now doth, like a garment, wear
The beauty of the morning; silent, bare,
Ships, towers, domes, theatres, and temples lie
Open unto the fields, and to the sky;
All bright and glittering in the smokeless air.
Never did sun more beautifully steep
In his first splendour, valley, rock, or hill;
Ne'er saw I, never felt, a calm so deep!
The river glideth at his own sweet will:
Dear God! the very houses seem asleep;
And all that mighty heart is lying still!

William Wordsworth (1770 – 1850)

The Night City

Unmet at Euston in a dream
Of London under Turner's steam
Misting the iron gantries, I
Found myself running away
From Scotland into the golden city.

I ran down Gray's Inn Road and ran
Till I was under a black bridge.
This was me at nineteen
Late at night arriving between
The buildings of the City of London.

And then I (O I have fallen down)
Fell in my dream beside the Bank
Of England's wall to bed, me
With my money belt of Northern ice.
I found Eliot and he said yes

And sprang into a Holmes cab.
Boswell passed me in the fog
Going to visit Whistler who
Was with John Donne who had just seen
Paul Potts shouting on Soho Green.

Midnight. I hear the moon
Light chiming on St Paul's.

The City is empty. Night
Watchmen are drinking their tea.

The Fire had burnt out.
The Plague's pits had closed
And gone into literature.

Between the big buildings
I sat like a flea crouched
In the stopped works of a watch.

WS Graham (1918 – 1986)

Underground

Riding down the moving stairs old fears
of severed feet, a sucked-in doll come back.
Commuters skip lightly off, a daily movement
perfected into an art. I still expect at least
my heel to catch, and stumble off, a beginner
yet again.

Beginning to die is familiar ground for me.
Start all over. You can make it a drama,
accept the worst, face it with dignity,
or say you don't approve, or even do it
yourself without the aid of life machine
or intensive care.

Standing carefully where I am, I trace
the blue Victoria line, remembering the wrong
directions I have taken and all the doors
I should have pushed, but pulled instead,
and all the men like you who took me
for a ride.

Riding still, I sit in my swaying carriage,
and wonder if I'm going North or South.
Am I right for King's Cross, I rehearse
to myself, but everyone seems to know just
where they're at, float to offices on time,
dive and swim.

Swimming through the corridors and past signs
I consider if the bow-wave of multi-coloured
faces are really fish and I am travelling
to be eaten whole, or piecemeal perhaps,
a passing shrimp, part of his daily meal
of fables.

Fabulous rescues like Mrs Bliss who thought
she'd had it off the coast of California,
until a warm snout nudged her to the shallows
place dolphins second only to man, who sport
in schools, but are seldom seen in this
underground oceanarium.

Is it an ocean or a city or a sea-bed?
Let's pretend. Put on your dolphin kit.
Look, it's a secret. Cross my heart
and hope to die, if ever I should tell
a lie. This is a magical kingdom if you have
half an ear or eye.

Elizabeth Bartlett (1924 – 2008)

Homecoming

The light is sullen today, yet people are
bustling in the rainy street under my window,

poking in the Cypriot grocers for aubergines,
buying their strings of garlic and onions;

they can choose between the many seeds on
the bread: rye, sesame, cumin.

Across the road, the pharmacy windows
are lettered in brass like a Victorian shop.

In the coffee house with its heavy green and gold
pottery, they serve bean soup with sausages

and the accents of old Vienna mingle
with California. In the countryside

every one of us would be found peculiar.
We'd leak away. In Englands Lane

(through road for taxis and the Camden hoppa)
this city music and a few friends keep me sane.

Elaine Feinstein (1930 – 2019)

A Linden Tree in a Whitechapel Street

Not in the countryside in a green field,
Spreading its branches wide,
With a flock of sheep sheltering under it,
With the shepherd at their side.

Not rooted in soft country soil,
With green fields all round,
But in a Whitechapel street,
In hard asphalted ground.

With his legs bound and his wings spread,
But never able to rise and fly,
The tree stands in this Whitechapel street.
And so do I.

Then suddenly the whole street is aflame.
There's a bird singing in the tree.
And somehow it seems to be singing
Also to me.

AN Stencl (1897 – 1983)
translated from the Yiddish by Joseph Leftwich

London

I wander thro' each charter'd street,
Near where the charter'd Thames does flow,
And mark in every face I meet
Marks of weakness, marks of woe.

In every cry of every Man,
In every Infant's cry of fear,
In every voice, in every ban,
The mind-forg'd manacles I hear.

How the Chimney-sweeper's cry
Every black'ning Church appalls;
And the hapless Soldier's sigh
Runs in blood down Palace walls.

But most thro' midnight streets I hear
How the youthful Harlot's curse
Blasts the new born Infant's tear,
And blights with plagues the Marriage hearse.

William Blake (1757 – 1827)

Two Rhymes for Children

Oranges and lemons,
Say the bells of St. Clement's.

You owe me five farthings,
Say the bells of St. Martin's.

When will you pay me?
Say the bells of Old Bailey.

When I grow rich,
Say the bells of Shoreditch.

When will that be?
Say the bells of Stepney.

I do not know,
Says the great bell of Bow.

Here comes a candle to light you to bed,
And here comes a chopper to chop off your head!

Traditional

See-saw, sacradown,
Which is the way to London town?
One foot up and the other foot down
That is the way to London town.

Traditional

Trojan Horse
London, thow art the flour of cities all – William Dunbar

New Troy cried Dunbar and so it was we entered
as if by stealth, wandering the suburbs
of her good pleasure, disorientated,
less an invading army than dizzy tourists
of our own helplessness, decentred,
tending to trip and stumble over kerbs,
our childish hands curled into childish fists,
our very strangeness oddly understated.

By the railway cuttings at Hendon we sat down
and thought how to weep when we remembered Zion,
but quite what Zion was we had forgotten.
The air we breathed contained a trace of it.
There was in the soil a particular shade of brown
that brought it back. Meanwhile the British lion
roared in the cinema so we should profit
from its power though the seats smelled rotten.

We stood in Trafalgar Square completely covered
in pigeons but looking all too pleased to find
such wholehearted acceptance. We were the boys
of the awkward squad, growing at an angle.
Occasionally perhaps one of us shivered
in the sheer tide of her, in the vast mind
of street-maps it took an alien to untangle,
as if she were not one but several Troys.

And sometimes now I see us as we were,
transported to the present, trying to keep warm
inside, selling Big Issues to ourselves,
sleeping in doorways even when in bed,
the street maps we know dissolving in a blur.
We're standing on an underground platform.
We're under Troy, tunnelling through her head,
riding without tickets, running with the wolves.

George Szirtes

The Capital

I stood on the steps of the National Gallery,
which rose like a temple above Trafalgar Square,
and watched the drama unfold like a tragedy:

the circus of black cabs everywhere,
people and pigeons and handouts of bread.
I walked past the Cenotaph's fallen dead.

A bronze general in Whitehall was riding a horse.
Officials in Ministries were filling out forms.
Politicians' statues in Parliament Square

wore togas, declaiming debates to the air,
and Old Father Thames, like the Tiber, wove home
past the embers of empire of Britain and Rome.

Sarah Wardle